RAINBOW REVOLUTIONARIES

• •

FOR ELEANOR AND MOLLIE, ALWAYS FOLLOW YOUR HEART —S. PRAGER

FOR EDNA, YOU FOLLOWED YOUR HEART —S. PAPWORTH

• •

Rainbow Revolutionaries: 50 LGBTQ+ People Who Made History

Text copyright © 2020 by Sarah Prager

Illustrations copyright © 2020 by Sarah Papworth

Map, symbols, and flags by Sara Franklin

All rights reserved. Manufactured in Spain.

ISBN 978-0-06-294775-8 (hardcover) — ISBN 978-0-06-309106-1 (paperback)

The artist used Adobe Photoshop along with textures made from watercolors, fine liners, pencils, and acrylics to create the digital illustrations for this book.

Book design by Alison Klapthor

23 24 25 26 27 LBC 6 5 4 3 2

❖

First Edition

RAINBOW REVOLUTIONARIES

50 LGBTQ+ PEOPLE WHO MADE HISTORY

WRITTEN BY SARAH PRAGER

ILLUSTRATED BY SARAH PAPWORTH

HARPER
An Imprint of HarperCollinsPublishers

CONTENTS

CONTENTS

NORTH AMERICA

ILLINOIS

MISSOURI
JOSEPHINE BAKER

KANSAS
ALAN L. HART
GILBERT BAKER

MARTINE ROTHBLATT

OHIO

CLEVE JONES
NATALIE CLIFFORD BARNEY
INDIANA
ADAM RIPPON
BAYARD RUSTIN

PENNSYLVANIA

HARVEY MILK,
CHRISTINE JORGENSEN,
JAMES BALDWIN,
RENEE RICHARDS, NEW YORK

SYLVIA RIVERA, NEW JERSEY
MARSHA P. JOHNSON,
BENJAMIN BANNEKER,
PAULI MURRAY, MARYLAND

BILLIE JEAN KING,
GLENN BURKE,
JOSÉ SARRIA,
SALLY RIDE

CALIFORNIA

WE'WHA

NEW MEXICO
TEXAS
ALVIN AILEY

STORME DELARVERIE,
ELLEN DEGENERES

GEORGIA
MA RAINEY

LOUISIANA

FRIDA KAHLO
JUANA INÉS DE LA CRUZ
MEXICO

BIRTHPLACES of the RAINBOW REVOLUTIONARIES

BRAZIL
ALBERTO SANTOS-DUMONT

SOUTH AMERICA

ICELAND

JÓHANNA SIGURÐARDÓTTIR

CHRISTINA OF SWEDEN,
GRETA GARBO

SWEDEN

UNITED KINGDOM

... CASHIER

ALAN TURING

LILI ELBE

DENMARK

FRIEDA BELINFANTE

THE NETHERLANDS

MAGNUS HIRSCHFELD

PRUSSIA (NOW POLAND)

EUROPE

CHEVALIÈRE D'ÉON,
JULIE D'AUBIGNY

FRANCE

MACEDON (NOW GREECE)

ALEXANDER THE GREAT

AL-HAKAM II

AL-ANDALUS (NOW SPAIN)

RUDOLF NUREYEV

SOVIET UNION (NOW RUSSIA)

ASIA

MARYAM KHATOON MOLKARA

IRAN

MANVENDRA SINGH GOHIL,
NAVTEJ JOHAR

WEN OF HAN

CHINA

INDIA

AFRICA

KONGO (NOW ANGOLA AND CONGO)

FRANCISCO MANICONGO

NDONGO AND MATAMBA (NOW ANGOLA)

NZINGA

TSHEPO RICKI KGOSITAU

BOTSWANA

SIMON NKOLI

SOUTH AFRICA

AUSTRALIA

GEORGINA BEYER

NEW ZEALAND

INTRODUCTION

When I was growing up, I didn't know that LGBTQ+ people had changed the world. I wrote this book to make sure you never have to think that.

Did you ever wonder who invented the computer? Or who invented the high five? Well, gay people invented both of those. And the technology that's in your tablet? That was a trans woman.

Yup, the world would be a really different place without computers or tablets or high fives, wouldn't it? The stories of those three inventors are in this book, along with the stories of a US Civil War soldier, a Mexican nun, and an Angolan queen. The first person to fly an airplane is in here, along with an astronaut from almost a hundred years later who flew a lot higher.

LGBTQ+ people have shaped the world as we know it. From conquerors to composers and artists to activists, the LGBTQ+ community has made a mark on every century of human existence.

This book is a celebration of fifty of the most inspiring and interesting LGBTQ+ people from throughout history. Those who are LGBTQ+ still have to keep who they are a secret in many parts of the world today, but in this book, no one is a secret. We can shout these names from the rooftops with pride.

When I was younger, I didn't learn the names or stories of any of these heroes. When I taught them to myself in high school, it changed my life. I knew I wasn't alone, I knew I wasn't the first to feel this way, I knew I could be anyone and achieve anything. I knew I was part of a big family.

After having my daughter while writing my first book, *Queer, There, and Everywhere*, I resolved to share the representation that book provided with a younger audience. I didn't see children's books celebrating the stories of my LGBTQ+ family, so I decided to create a collection of fifty true stories of people from around the world and across time who everyone should know about.

These biographies are meant to give you a sense of how many different ways LGBTQ+ people have made a difference . . . and how you can make a difference, too.

ADAM

RIPPON

1989-Present
UNITED STATES

ADAM RIPPON

Adam was born knowing how to be first. He was the first of six kids in his family in rural Pennsylvania . . . and he would go on to be first many other times in his life.

An active kid, he just wasn't clicking with any sports he tried . . . until he found ice skating when he was ten. It quickly became a passion, and he started winning medals at various competitions.

But there was more to Adam's identity than ice skating. . . . He'd known he was gay since he was little. He struggled with it for a long time, not wanting to come out to himself, let alone to others. The first time he told someone he was gay, it was like a huge weight being lifted off his shoulders. He said he felt "reborn." When he came out to the whole world in 2015, it was a big deal for an American male athlete. He says that even if you're not LGBTQ+, sharing who you are with the world and coming out as *yourself* can make you powerful. Amen!

In 2018 he became the first ever openly gay US athlete to qualify for a Winter Olympics. Later that year in South Korea, he became the first openly gay US athlete to win a medal at a Winter Olympics!

His BFF mother raised her children to believe they were champions. Adam ended up an Olympic champion, but he says that being a champion "is more than a medal. It's a mind-set." Anyone can be a champion by being themselves—yes, that means you!

ALAN L. HART

1890 - 1962
UNITED STATES

ALAN L. HART

Alan really loved his grandparents. Some of us have a special fondness for Grandma and Grandpa because of their cookies or hugs, but for Alan, his affection came from something else.

When he was at his grandparents' farm in Oregon growing up, Alan got to dress and act like a boy. Alan was always a boy, but because he was assigned female at birth, he had to wait until he was grown up before he got the chance to present as a man full-time. His grandparents always respected young Alan as a grandson no matter what others thought.

After being forced to attend school and college presenting as a girl, as an adult Alan became the first person in the US to transition with the help of medical doctors. He learned from what **Magnus Hirschfeld** had done for another trans man in Germany and got an American doctor to help. By 1918 he'd had gender affirming surgery and been able to legally change his name to Alan. In 1925, he married his second wife, Edna Ruddick, and they were together the rest of Alan's life. Aww!

Now, a hundred years ago, people didn't have the medical advances we have today, not just for gender transition, but also in terms of helping people who got sick. The number one cause of death in the US was a disease called tuberculosis (TB). Since there was no cure, the most important thing for someone with TB was to discover it early to get treatment. But there was a big problem—diagnosing it in the early stages was really hard.

Alan became a doctor and turned into a leader in the TB field. He pioneered use of the new X-ray technology to find TB early, meaning that doctors could now find the disease in people in time to treat it before it got too serious. Because of Alan's work, deaths by TB plummeted dramatically. He saved countless lives! Alan was a true pioneer . . . in more ways than one.

ALAN TURING

1912 – 1954
UNITED KINGDOM

ALAN TURING

World War II was raging across Europe. Alan was an academic, not a soldier. So what could he do to help his country of Britain?

Alan had completed advanced studies in a new field that we know today as computer science, but in the 1940s there was no such thing as a computer. No smartphones, no laptops, no tablets—nothing with a glowing screen.

The Nazis (the enemy in the war) had a secret code they used to write to each other called the Enigma code. No human had been able to crack the code and figure out how to translate it. If the British could read what the Nazis were telling each other, they could win the war!

So immediately when the British entered the war, Alan joined a team of very smart people who began working on a way to break the Enigma code. What Alan ended up inventing with his team was the world's first computer. It could automatically check all the possible answers to the Enigma riddle and solve it. Alan called it his universal machine.

With the universal machine, the British and their allies went on to beat the Nazis and win World War II! Alan had made a huge difference, and he went back to his life of studying more about computers.

There was a problem, though. Alan was a man who loved other men, and it was illegal to do that in 1950s Britain. When the police found out, they arrested Alan, and his punishment was forced medical treatment that was supposed to make him stop loving men. That is impossible to do, so it didn't work, and it made Alan miserable. He died just two years later, without anyone knowing about his top secret work that helped to save thousands of lives.

In 2013, the Queen of England officially pardoned Alan for his "crime" of loving another man (which is no longer illegal in Britain). Now that the public knows about what he did during the war, he is famous, loved, and appreciated all over the whole world. He gave us all a huge gift that changed everything. Think of Alan the next time you're on your universal machine—aka tablet!

ALBERT

1843 – 1915
IRELAND / US

CASHIER

ALBERT CASHIER

Albert was about to change his life forever, but it seemed impossible without ten dollars.

Ten dollars is how much a ticket for a boat to take him from Ireland to America cost—and Albert didn't have ten dollars. Not even close. So Albert stowed away on the ship without a ticket. And got away with it!

Albert made it to America and started his new life. It wasn't just a new place that made it a new life—Albert had made a big change when he took that boat ride. In Ireland he had always presented as a woman, but he took off his dress in the port in Ireland and never looked back. It was his chance to be himself.

But there was trouble in his new country—war. Albert joined the army (he did need a job) and fought for the North in the Civil War. He fought bravely for three years. Once, he was captured by Southern soldiers, but he escaped. Another time, he ran out into the middle of a battle to save an American flag. Albert was a great soldier, a true hero.

Everyone always respected him as a man, even after the war. Before he died in old age, someone discovered his assigned-female body. His soldier friends came to make sure Albert was buried with his rightful name on the headstone and in his military uniform . . . and he was.

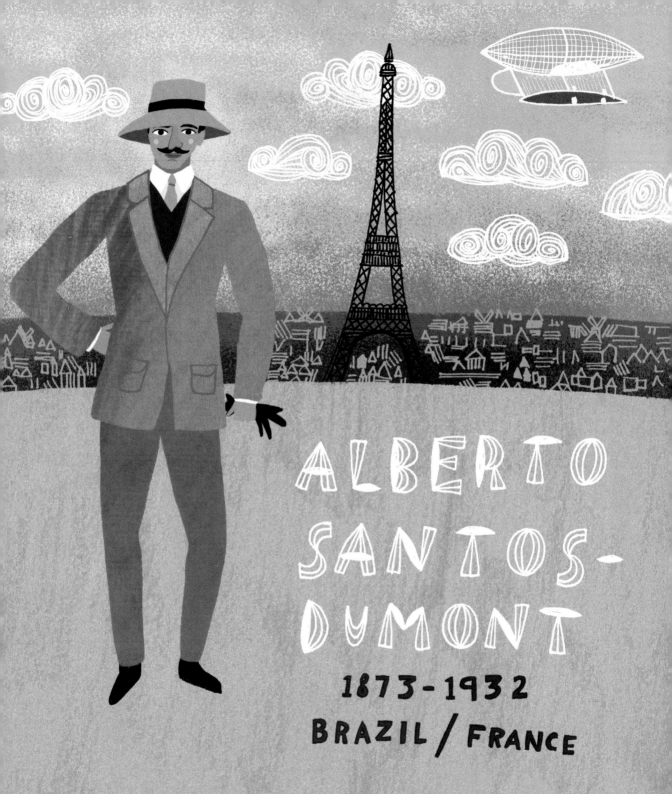

ALBERTO SANTOS-DUMONT

1873-1932

BRAZIL / FRANCE

ALBERTO SANTOS-DUMONT

Alberto always dreamed of flying. He'd stare up at the clouds as a kid in Brazil and imagine himself up there with them. His love of flying was only matched by his love of tinkering with machines, like the ones that processed the beans at the coffee plantation where he grew up.

Around his nineteenth birthday, Alberto made the big move to live in Paris, France. He had heard Paris was a place of great innovation at this time, with new creations like cars and hot air balloons. He was not disappointed. Alberto was in the right place to be an inventor and started making flying machines right away.

He was known for making the huge step from inventing contraptions that allowed humans to float or glide through the air to ones that allowed them to fly with control by adding a car motor to his airships. He would experiment with one machine and crash to the ground inside it, somehow not ever injuring himself too seriously. He never let fear overtake him, like the time he repaired his machine just in the nick of time by stepping outside his basket onto a wing two thousand feet in the air. You never knew if he might plow into your backyard or float down to park his airship with the bicycles to go into a restaurant. He was quite a celebrity around Paris.

The press was confused by him: one side was a daring, brave engineer, and the other side was someone feminine who loved knitting and tea parties. Alberto never had any romantic relationships that we know of—his only love was flying.

In 1900, a wealthy man named Henri Deutsch created a contest: whoever could fly from a certain point in Paris, circle the Eiffel Tower, and land back at the first point within thirty minutes would win a prize. Alberto was determined to win, but the first time he tried, he failed. The second time, he ended up on top of a hotel roof! Alberto wouldn't give up, but during his third attempt, his engine stalled and he had to fix it. Then it stalled again and he fixed it again, and then again a third time. Every delay cost him precious moments, but he made it back to the starting point twenty-nine minutes and fifteen seconds after takeoff. He had done it!

Alberto followed his dreams no matter what and wouldn't give up. He was the first person to ever fly a heavier-than-air aircraft in public . . . even before the Wright brothers!

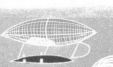

ALEXANDER

356 – 323 BC
GREECE

THE GREAT

14

ALEXANDER THE GREAT

You never know when a baby is born what they'll grow up to be. Maybe an artist, maybe a philosopher, maybe a construction worker . . . or conqueror of most of the known world?

Alexander wasn't born Alexander the Great—he earned that title. Alexander III of Macedon was born in northern Greece and educated by the incredible Aristotle, now considered the father of Western philosophy.

Alexander's dad, the king of Macedon, died when Alexander was twenty, making Alexander king. He set out to become much more than that, waging one successful military campaign after another. Over the next ten years he became pharaoh of Egypt, king of Persia, and lord of Asia! He created one of the largest empires in all of human history, ruling from Greece to India. Alexander, who loved both men and women, never lost a battle!

Many conquerors were very unkind to the people on the land they took control of, but Alexander was against taking slaves and forcing women to get married. When food came in for the troops, he made sure everyone else ate first, even if nothing was left for him. He was respected as a fair ruler. What kind of ruler do you think you'd be?

915-976
SPAIN

AL-HAKAM II

AL-HAKAM II

Al-Andalus (part of modern-day Spain) was one of the most powerful empires in the world a thousand years ago . . . and Al-Hakam II was its ruler.

Al-Hakam was raised to be a leader. He had plenty of time to practice, too—he didn't rise to the throne until he was forty-six. His dad raised him to keep practicing and practicing how to run a kingdom, and it really paid off.

Al-Hakam brought Al-Andalus to the peak of its splendor. He made peace with the Christians to the north, defeated the Vikings by sea, and conquered Morocco to the south. He put a focus on education, creating over two dozen new public schools. He created an enormous library with thousands of books from all over the world and led a great translation campaign. He took on the construction of incredible, beautiful buildings, including the famous Mosque of Córdoba, which people from around the world come to see today.

But there was a problem. Just as his father had passed on Al-Andalus to him, Al-Hakam needed a son to pass on the kingdom to. Al-Hakam didn't have a wife (or want one), but he needed to have a child. So he had a woman dress up like a man, and they made a baby so that Al-Andalus could have a future ruler.

One of the most important parts of Al-Hakam's reign was that he treated people with respect and equality, whether they were Muslims, Jews, or Christians. This was especially a big deal over a thousand years ago! Spain and the world (maybe even your school!) are still enjoying the investments of his reign today.

ALVIN AILEY

1931 - 1989
UNITED STATES

ALVIN AILEY

Men don't dance.

That's the message Alvin got growing up. Thankfully, his high school teachers encouraged him to dance anyway.

Alvin was mesmerized when he first saw professional dancing in LA after moving from Texas. His single mom had moved them there for a job, since work was hard to find for a black woman during the Depression in the South. A big city, away from the white robes of the KKK openly parading through their hometown, held promise for the family of two.

Alvin wasn't going to mess this up. Once, he had a group of friends who were going to rob a store, but he stood up to them and said no (even though he was so nervous it took him several minutes to work up the courage to say it). He decided he was going to commit his life to positive things.

Alvin took gymnastics in high school, and his coach suggested that he try dancing. He loved it! Everyone else in his dance class had been dancing since they were really little, so he had to learn fast as an older teenager. He worked hard, and a man named Lester Horton, who was also gay like Alvin, became his dance mentor.

Alvin danced in Lester's racially integrated dance troupe starting in 1953. Sadly, Lester passed away that same year. Even though he was so new to dancing, Alvin stepped up and began choreographing pieces for the dance company. Eventually he moved to New York City to start his own multiracial group, the Alvin Ailey American Dance Theater, in 1958. That troupe is still in operation today (over sixty years later!), and the group is considered a cultural ambassador to the world.

Alvin's most famous dance work, *Revelations*, has been seen by millions of people in dozens of countries on six continents. It is possibly the most often seen piece of modern dance in the world! Not bad for a kid "late" to dance.

BAYARD RUSTIN

1912 – 1987
UNITED STATES

20

BAYARD RUSTIN

You've heard of Rosa Parks and Martin Luther King Jr., right? Well, did you know that thirteen years before Rosa refused to change her seat on that bus, there was someone else doing the same thing? And that Martin had a lot of help behind the scenes?

Bayard Rustin was one of the Freedom Riders, a group of black and white people who disobeyed the segregation laws on Southern buses by riding together in the front, which was reserved for white people only. They were arrested and beaten for what they did, but they knew defying the unjust law was the right thing to do.

In 1948, Bayard traveled to India to learn about the nonviolence of Mahatma Gandhi and became convinced this strategy was the best way for the US civil rights movement to succeed. He believed in it with all his heart.

The movement's leaders thought nonviolent tactics might seem weak and didn't want to try them, but Bayard kept doing what he thought was right. He got arrested all the time for refusing to follow unfair laws, but that didn't stop him. Bayard eventually became the trusted adviser of Dr. Martin Luther King Jr., and Bayard convinced Martin that nonviolence was the way to go. It was a huge win!

Bayard was a lead organizer of the 1963 March on Washington, where Martin told the crowd of 250,000 of his dream. Bayard spoke at that march, too, and made the cover of *Time* magazine. Lots of people march on Washington now, but nothing like this had ever been accomplished before 1963. With racial and police tensions high, Bayard pulled off an amazing feat by keeping the march peaceful.

At the age of sixty-five, Bayard finally met his life partner, Walter Naegle. Walter and Bayard became activists for LGBTQ+ civil rights for the rest of their lives. When President Barack Obama awarded Bayard the Presidential Medal of Freedom in 2013, after Bayard had passed away, Walter was there to receive it for him.

Did you ever make the choice to stand up for what you believe in no matter what?

BENJAMIN BANNEKER

★ 1731 – 1806
UNITED STATES

BENJAMIN BANNEKER

When Benjamin was a young man, he built a wooden clock that actually kept correct time for the rest of his life. He wasn't taught how to do it (and he didn't even own a clock!) . . . he just . . . did it. That's the kind of mind Benjamin had. It led him to astronomy, the study of insects, calculations about land, and every science in between.

Benjamin was born in Maryland to farmers: an African American mother and a father who was forcefully brought to the US as a slave from Guinea. Benjamin didn't ever really go to much school . . . but that doesn't mean he wasn't learning. He taught himself all kinds of things, just like how to make the clock. In 1788 he began making calculations about the planets, and in 1789 he correctly predicted a solar eclipse!

Benjamin, who didn't have any documented romantic relationships his whole life, put his mind to use on a team making the original borders of the city of Washington, DC. He had to use a lot of math he had taught himself, and it paid off when they successfully laid out the one hundred square miles on the ground they set out to do.

There's much more science that Benjamin impressively accomplished, but another really cool thing he did was write to Thomas Jefferson asking for justice for African Americans. At the time (1791), Tom was just secretary of state, not yet president, but he was very important as an author of the Declaration of Independence. Thomas Jefferson owned slaves, and Benjamin called him out on it. How could Tom write about freedom while participating in the oppression of fellow humans? Benjamin included a copy of the almanac he had written to get Tom's attention, and it worked. Tom Jefferson wrote back that he agreed black people should have better conditions.

Benjamin used his intellect not only to form his country's capital city but to advocate for his people's rights. Ace job!

1943-Present
UNITED STATES

24

BILLIE JEAN KING

*F*rom the moment she first picked up a tennis racket in fifth grade, Billie Jean knew she wanted to be a tennis player for life. She set a goal to become the number one tennis player in the world.

Billie Jean achieved her goal and was number one in the world for women's tennis *six* different years in the 1960s and 1970s. Wow! Not only that, but she has thirty-nine Grand Slam titles to her name and has won Wimbledon a record-setting twenty times. She is known not only for being one of the tennis world's major champions, but for her work for equality.

When she won the US Open in 1972, she received less prize money than the men's winner. This was completely unfair! Billie Jean wouldn't stand for it and advocated for equal pay. Because of the hard work of herself and others, the US Open became the first major tennis tournament in the world to offer equal prize money to women and men!

Not everyone believed men and women tennis players were equal. One male player, Bobby Riggs, said men were better players than women and even that men were superior outside of tennis too. Billie Jean said NO WAY! He challenged her to play a game against him. At first, she didn't want to do it, but she eventually agreed.

Everyone was talking about this game, which became known as the Battle of the Sexes. The pressure was high, and Billie Jean knew that people would judge all women athletes on how she performed. Ninety million people watched as she *won* against Bobby and scored a victory for women everywhere in the most watched tennis game of all time.

But Billie Jean had a secret—she was a lesbian. LGBTQ+ people weren't much accepted during the 1970s, and coming out would have meant losing so much—like her tennis career itself. Someone outed Billie Jean in 1981 before she was ready to come out herself. She said it was the darkest time of her life.

Billie Jean overcame this too and went on to have a happy life. She has been with her partner, Ilana Kloss, for over thirty years, and together they mentor young tennis players of all backgrounds to get involved in the sport they love. They even helped Venus and Serena Williams get started in tennis when they were little!

CHEVALIÈRE d'EON

CHEVALIÈRE D'ÉON

Charles-Geneviève-Louis-Auguste-André-Timothée d'Éon de Beaumont had charm, wit, bravery . . . and a really long name, which is why she's remembered by history simply as Chevalier (which means "Sir") d'Éon. We'll just call her Charles.

Charles, assigned male at birth, took a job with the French government as secretary to the ambassador to Russia in 1756. But this was just a cover! Her *real* job was in the king's secret spy organization to gain the trust of the Russian court to carry out whatever France wanted.

She next lived as a spy in England from 1762 to 1777. She was officially a French ambassador to the English court, but she really was checking out the English coast to find places where France could attack! She presented as male almost this whole time until she was forty-nine, and then she made the public transition to female.

On November 21, 1777, Charles was formally presented to the French court at Versailles as a woman, Mademoiselle la *Chevalière* d'Éon. No one had ever had their transition accepted at court before! Charles got dressed for the occasion by Marie Antoinette's stylist (a task that took four hours), and Queen Marie even gave Charles a whole new women's wardrobe.

CHRISTINA

OF SWEDEN

1626 – 1689
SWEDEN

CHRISTINA OF SWEDEN

All their life, Christina had been destined to be queen of their country. Running the country of Sweden became Christina's job when they were six, and it was a lot of hard work. Thankfully they loved the work . . . and they were good at it! They even brought peace to Europe by ending the Thirty Years' War.

Unfortunately, there was a rule that queens *had* to get married to men. Christina couldn't be queen without getting married, but that was the one thing Christina never *ever* wanted to do. Christina even said, "I'd rather choose death than a man."

So at the age of twenty-six, Christina quit being queen. Yes, really! They took off on horseback and traveled as a male, leaving behind all the power and wealth, to live a free life. Now Christina didn't have to get married, and this made them happy.

Christina dressed in men's clothes and women's clothes, acted mostly like a man, and loved men and women. Living in Rome after leaving Sweden, this brave person lived life on their own terms and no one else's. Christina believed you should live your life the way you want no matter what others think—so that's what they did. How would you live if you could do that too?

CHRISTINE JORGENSEN

1929 – 1989
UNITED STATES

CHRISTINE JORGENSEN

Growing up in the Bronx (with twenty-six aunts, uncles, and cousins in the neighborhood!), Christine never imagined she'd one day be the most famous woman in the US for a moment. She wasn't even sure she was a girl yet.

It wasn't until the years after high school that Christine started reading up on the very limited information out there in the 1940s on gender identity (pretty much one book). Christine was raised as and seen as a boy, though she came to understand that she was a woman.

Christine stayed within what was expected of males (including serving a year in the military) through her early twenties in large part not to upset her family. What she really wanted was to be a photographer, so after the army, she took a bus from New York to Los Angeles with just a camera and $500, hoping for a Hollywood break.

When she began her transition from male to female, she sent a letter home from California to her parents explaining. To her surprise, her whole family was supportive, even her grandmother! They even loaned her money for hormone therapy.

Christine's life changed forever when she found a doctor in Denmark who was offering gender affirmation surgeries. Such surgeries were still tough to find, and she sailed to Copenhagen in 1950 for several operations spread over two years. She was so grateful for the procedures that she chose her name "Christine" in honor of her doctor, Christian Hamburger.

On December 1, 1952, hundreds of thousands of people read about Christine's story in a newspaper article headlined "Ex-GI Becomes Blonde Beauty." Reporters flocked to tell her story. She was her generation's only trans celebrity!

Christine was the first person in the US to describe herself so publicly as trans. Maybe today she would have had her own TV show!

CLEVE JONES

1954–Present
UNITED STATES

CLEVE JONES

Cleve felt lost and alone when he discovered he was gay in 1960s Arizona. He was miserable until one day in 1971, when he saw a magazine that had an article about the gay rights movement. Everything changed for him once he knew there were others out there like him. He held on to that magazine like he was clinging to dear life.

When he was eighteen, Cleve moved to San Francisco, a place he had read about in the magazine as a place for his people. The article was right. That foggy city in California quickly became a home for Cleve and other runaways.

When men in San Francisco started getting sick in 1983, Cleve was concerned. More and more men who loved men were coming down with a rare form of often-fatal cancer. Cleve was scared as many gay and bisexual men started dying—his friends were disappearing. For over a decade, more than a thousand people a year died of what we now call HIV/AIDS in San Francisco. Cleve got sick too but survived. The government wasn't helping to come up with a cure for this disease, and Cleve wanted to do something that would bring the epidemic to everyone's attention and get help.

One night at a march in San Francisco, Cleve got an idea. He had everyone write down the name of someone they had lost to HIV/AIDS. *Everyone* knew someone. They put the names up on the wall of city hall, and when Cleve looked at it, he thought it looked familiar . . . like a quilt.

A quilt! Something everyone could relate to. Something that reminds people of their grandmothers. Something made up of diverse scraps. Something that feels comforting and personal. What Cleve did next touched millions of lives.

He made the first panels of a quilt and then organized *thousands* of other panels to be made. Each one is a memorial to a person who died of HIV/AIDS. The quilt is now so big it weighs fifty-four *tons*. The NAMES Project AIDS Memorial Quilt was displayed five times on the National Mall in Washington, DC, and President Bill Clinton and First Lady Hillary Clinton came to see it in 1996. It was the biggest community arts project ever made, and it helped personalize an epidemic that changed the LGBTQ+ community forever.

The fight for people living with HIV/AIDS isn't over, and Cleve isn't stopping anytime soon.

Ellen

1958-Present
UNITED STATES

DeGeneres

ELLEN DEGENERES

Coming out was scary for Ellen, because it meant she could lose everything. She was a successful actress and comedian, and it seemed no one in Hollywood was out. If she told people she was a lesbian, she could lose her job and all future jobs. Not to mention her friends, safety, and who knows what else!

She had a dream one night about a bird who realized the cage it was in had been up against an open window all along, with the bars wide enough for it to fly out. She looked at the bird and asked it to stay inside because it was safe. But the bird looked at her and said, "I don't belong in here," and flew out.

After she had that dream, she knew she had to come out. It was a huge risk, but staying in the closet meant living half a life as someone who wasn't herself. She didn't belong in there. So in 1997, Ellen had the character (also named Ellen) on her TV show come out as a lesbian. It would have been pretty much impossible for Ellen's character to come out without Ellen coming out in real life, so she did that too.

Sometimes coming out means telling your family and friends you're LGBTQ+ (Ellen had already done that years ago). When you're famous, it means going on the cover of *Time* magazine next to the words "Yep, I'm Gay!" Quite the coming-out!

And Ellen did lose everything, as she had feared. Homophobia in the TV industry and in the American public got her TV show canceled the year after the coming-out episode. Ellen didn't find work again for THREE YEARS. They were a long three years for her. But then something wonderful happened . . . she started to get work again. Her career not only recovered—it came back better than ever.

Her talk show, *Ellen*, has been going since 2003 and has millions upon millions of adoring fans. She has a loving wife, Portia de Rossi, who she married legally in 2008, and together they live with their many pets. Flying free as a bird, Ellen, by taking a risk, not only made her own life happier but served as inspiration for countless other LGBTQ+ people to come out.

FRANCISCO

MANICONGO

1500s
ANGOLA/BRAZIL

36

FRANCISCO MANICONGO

*F*rancisco grew up in a part of Africa that is Angola and the Congo today. He was a "jimbandaa," a person assigned male at birth who loved men and dressed as a woman. Jimbandaas were honored in their community as special people. When slavers took Francisco, he was sent on a terrible journey across the Atlantic Ocean. Many people died on this voyage, but Francisco survived and arrived in Brazil.

In Brazil, Francisco became seen as the property of a shoemaker. No one saw Francisco as a human being anymore; just as a slave who had no rights. Francisco wouldn't accept this. He refused to wear the Brazilian men's clothing they gave him, because at home he dressed in special feminine jimbandaa clothes, and he would not stop being true to himself.

What happened to Francisco after that? He got in trouble for refusing to wear the clothes, but the story of what happened next has been lost to history. He is a fierce example of how someone can stand up for themselves no matter the circumstances. Francisco had everything on the line when he decided to fight back nonviolently, and he showed courage in the face of oppression.

"I'M HAPPY TO BE ALIVE AS LONG AS I CAN PAINT."

FRIDA KAHLO

1907 – 1954 · MEXICO

FRIDA KAHLO

*F*rida was a troublemaking prankster as a teenager, but something changed her life completely when she was eighteen.

Frida was with her boyfriend, Alejandro, riding the bus, when a streetcar smashed into them. A handrail injured Frida so badly that she broke many bones, including her spine. She spent a month in a hospital unable to move at all!

After the accident, Frida needed a lot of surgeries and had to spend *a lot* of time in bed. She would lie there, alone and bored, until one day her parents brought her painting supplies. Using a mirror, she would paint self-portraits while in bed.

When she was able to walk again, she took her paintings to show to a famous Mexican painter, Diego Rivera. He liked them, and she started a career as a painter . . . and a life as Diego's girlfriend and then wife. Frida loved men and women but only ever married Diego.

Frida's career as a painter grew, though her husband was more famous. She became well-known for her self-portraits, which always featured her signature unibrow. Eventually she made a name for herself as an artist, and her work was even displayed in the Louvre in Paris.

Frida was in pain much of her life due to the accident, and she expressed herself through her art, portraying herself sometimes as broken, but always strong.

1904-1995

The Netherlands / US

FRIEDA BELINFANTE

FRIEDA BELINFANTE

*F*rieda came from a musical family in Amsterdam, the Netherlands, and started playing cello when she was ten. Her sister says that because Frieda had small hands, she had to wrestle to handle the large instrument. Frieda conquered the cello just like she took on other difficulties in life.

Frieda, who was a lesbian, got the chance to try her hand at something else musical besides the cello—conducting. There she found her true passion. She was so talented at conducting student musicians that she got the opportunity to conduct a professional orchestra. Her friends were skeptical that she could pull it off—no woman had ever conducted a professional orchestra before in Europe! In 1937 Frieda tried . . . and succeeded.

But Frieda had to disband her orchestra in 1940 because of World War II. Frieda put her steady hands to work by forging fake identity documents for Jews. At that time in the Netherlands, the Nazis were trying to find all the Jewish people. Everyone was required to carry identification, so Frieda made documents for Jewish people to carry that said they weren't Jewish, so they could escape. It was dangerous work, but Frieda knew it was the right thing to do.

She even helped plan a bombing of Amsterdam's city hall so that all the original IDs were destroyed and Jewish people would be protected. After the bombing, in 1943, Frieda had to go into hiding. The Nazis captured many of the activists she had worked with on the attack, but Frieda disguised herself as a man and was able to go undetected for weeks. Her male look was so convincing that her own mother didn't recognize her when she passed her on the street. Then Frieda escaped to Switzerland, crossing snowy mountains and fording icy rivers (even though she couldn't swim) to get to a place where she could survive.

After the war, Frieda wanted a new life, so she moved to Southern California—somewhere to warm her heart after all the horrors she had seen. Years after her orchestra had been ended by the war, she got the chance to be a conductor again, this time with the Orange County Philharmonic until 1962. She spent her life breaking barriers in music and heroically helping people in need.

GEORGINA
BEYER

1957–Present
NEW ZEALAND

GEORGINA BEYER

Georgina Beyer was assigned male at birth but would dress like a girl in secret every chance she got. She was punished whenever she got caught, but as she grew, so did her daring. Georgina would dress like a girl in public and eventually made the transition to presenting only as a young woman when she was sixteen. She didn't have the support of her family at the time, but she found friends who accepted her, and, most important, she accepted herself.

Georgina had a tough early life, but then she found something she really loved and was really good at: being an actress! She played many different roles on TV before moving to a small, rural, conservative town called Carterton in the Wairarapa region of New Zealand. She began to be a part of the community as a drama teacher and community center manager and eventually was elected to city council. Just like that she went from actress to politician . . . but she didn't stop there.

Next she set her sights on becoming mayor of Carterton. Would this town elect a woman who was open about her transsexual identity? She wasn't sure, but she decided to try. And then something amazing happened . . . she won the race!

Georgina became the first out trans mayor of any town anywhere in 1995. The first ever! Not to mention she was also Carterton's first female mayor and their first mayor of Maori descent. She was very proud, and she loved her new job. She made getting young people involved in the political process a priority of her mayoralty. In 1999, she took a huge step and ran for Parliament. This wasn't just representing a small town; this was breaking onto the national stage! No one thought she would win, but she had a surprise victory, becoming the first out trans member of parliament anywhere in the world. *The first ever!*

It wasn't easy, but Georgina got to a place where she had a big influence over policies that affected her life. She had a chance as a member of Parliament to speak up for many communities, including the LGBTQ+ community, when New Zealand voted to allow same-sex civil unions in 2004. As Georgina said, "out of adversity and against all the odds can come triumph."

1951 - 2017
UNITED STATES

GILBERT
BAKER

GILBERT BAKER

*D*o you know the word "vexillographer"? It's time to learn.

Gilbert Baker was a vexillographer—a flag maker. He made flags and banners for political events, for antiwar protests, for rock concerts, for all kinds of things. But in June 1978, he made his most important flag—the rainbow flag.

Gilbert grew up in Kansas and wanted to get out of there. He joined the army and was stationed as a medic in San Francisco and found a home there, staying after his service and living as an openly gay man. He became part of the community that included **Harvey Milk**—a community asking for a symbol.

Gilbert stayed up for nights on end dying fabric and sewing it together. Volunteers helped him as they made the first Pride flag. It flew in San Francisco with eight colors, each one with meaning like "nature" or "healing." After dropping two of the colors due to high production costs, Gilbert's creation became known as a symbol for the LGBTQ+ community around the whole world, used in countless ways.

In 1994, Gilbert made a rainbow flag that was a whole mile long to celebrate the twenty-fifth anniversary of the Stonewall Rebellion. He unfurled it in New York City—well, he and the five thousand people it took to carry it. It broke a world record for the longest flag!

Gilbert never trademarked the flag, so it belongs to the public. The rainbow flag is truly the most iconic, recognizable symbol of the LGBTQ+ community, and we all owe a debt to Gilbert for creating something so unifying and empowering.

Glenn Burke

1952 – 1995
UNITED STATES

GLENN BURKE

Glenn always loved sports, but he also always loved men. Being out as gay at the same time as being a professional athlete in the 1970s was almost impossible. Glenn had to hide who he was in order to live out his dream—playing Major League Baseball.

Glenn reached his dream in 1976, when he joined the Los Angeles Dodgers. One of the team's managers, Tommy Lasorda, was homophobic—and also had a gay son, Spunky. Glenn and Spunky became close and loved going to the Castro, an LGBTQ+ neighborhood in San Francisco, but Tommy disapproved of their relationship. Glenn was playing well for the team, but his career was in danger for something that had nothing to do with his baseball talent.

While playing for the Dodgers, Glenn did something unique that would impact millions of people—he co-invented the high five! Isn't it funny to think about a time before the high five existed? Well, the one that started it all was between Glenn and a teammate, Dusty Baker, during a game in 1977. Dusty said that when Glenn put his hand up, hitting it just "seemed like the thing to do." It became a baseball tradition, then popular in all sports, and then second nature everywhere as it is today.

When he was called into the Dodgers' general manager's office one day, Glenn assumed it was to discuss renewing his contract. Instead, he was offered an ultimatum: marry a woman or else. The general manager offered Glenn $75,000 if he would marry a woman, any woman, but Glenn refused. Shortly after, Glenn was traded to another team and then forced into early retirement at age twenty-six.

In 1982, he appeared on the national *Today* show to talk openly about being gay. It was the first time any athlete had ever done that on American television! Glenn was a pioneer many years before any other athlete would come out publicly.

GRETA GARBO

1905–1990
SWEDEN/US

GRETA GARBO

Greta Garbo was one of the first superstars in the 1920s and 1930s, greeted by screaming fans whenever the news reported where she'd be. Unfortunately, this didn't mesh with Greta's private persona. Instead of waving to the fans, she'd put a magazine in front of her face and try to get away. She would even wear disguises and use fake names when she was in public.

Growing up in Sweden, Greta had always wanted to be an actress, and she was accepted to acting school there at the age of sixteen. She was one of only ten who got in out of three hundred who applied! She moved to the US at the age of nineteen, ready to become a star (maybe without fully realizing what that would involve).

And she did it! Greta had her first hit movie at the age of twenty. And guess what: She played **Christina of Sweden** in a 1933 movie called *Queen Christina*! In it, she wore men's clothing and kissed a woman on the lips!

But Greta didn't just kiss other women when she was acting. In real life, she loved men and women, including New York City writer Mercedes de Acosta. Mercedes was the one who sent Greta to her tailor, and when Greta walked out of the shop wearing pants, women everywhere wanted to ditch their dresses and dress like the actress.

Greta may have appeared cold and icy because she was so private, but she really just wanted to be an actress because she loved acting, not for the fame. She was extremely talented and dedicated to her roles, and many of her twenty-eight films were successes—she earned three Oscar nominations for Best Actress. No matter how famous she became, she was always shrouded in mystery.

HARVEY MILK

1930 - 1978
UNITED STATES

"YOU HAVE TO GIVE PEOPLE HOPE"

HARVEY MILK

Growing up in New York, Harvey Milk never imagined he would change the world. Along with his brother, Harvey helped out at the family's department store, Milk's. It was only after he moved to San Francisco that he saw a lot of discrimination. Many people there treated others who didn't look or act just like them differently, and Harvey didn't like it!

Harvey made his home in a neighborhood called the Castro and started a camera shop . . . even though he knew nothing about photography! As a gay man, Harvey liked that the Castro was becoming a neighborhood filled with people just like him.

Still, Harvey wanted to change the discrimination he saw. The government and police weren't treating gay people like him fairly. So Harvey decided to run for office! People held signs and wore buttons with his name on them, including Harvey's intern **Cleve Jones**. Harvey wanted to be part of the Board of Supervisors, who make decisions about how things should be in San Francisco. An openly gay person had never been part of the city government before, but Harvey thought the people of the Castro deserved a representative like them.

He didn't win the election. He ran again and lost a second time. But Harvey persisted and finally won in 1977! As part of San Francisco's Board of Supervisors, he helped to make laws that treated everyone fairly. The gay people of San Francisco finally had a voice. He was one of the very first openly gay people ever elected to government in the United States.

Sadly, Harvey's first year in office was also his last. A man with hate in his heart ended Harvey's life. But even Harvey's death helped people. People came together to make sure Harvey's work for equality continued.

Harvey gave people hope, and that hope never died.

JAMES BALDWIN

1924 – 1987
US/FRANCE

JAMES BALDWIN

James was a great writer in high school in the Harlem neighborhood of New York City, but when he graduated, he had to put college on hold. He needed to work laying railroad track to help support his family, which included seven younger siblings. Eventually, he ended up beginning to make money off his writing . . . and followed that path right to becoming one of the greatest writers of the twentieth century.

James wrote and wrote and wrote, yet struggled to be seen as more than a black writer. He wanted to be seen simply as a *writer*, judged for his talent, but the public kept putting him in a box.

Instead of backing down, James (who was bi) went ahead and wrote *Giovanni's Room*, a book with gay and bi characters. He didn't tell anyone he was going to write it, so when he handed in this surprise book to his US publishers, they were not happy. They told him he was a black writer needing to write about the black experience, and gay/bi topics were separate. They didn't see black and LGBTQ+ as being possible together. Not to mention how controversial it would be to publish something with gayness and bisexuality in it in the first place.

James didn't give up. He brought his book to other publishers and got it published in 1956. Even though people went from seeing him as a black writer to seeing him as an LGBTQ+ writer, he was still trapped in a box. But no matter what, James wrote about what he knew without apologizing.

After spending almost ten years living in France to escape US racial prejudices, James came home to confront them. He toured the South speaking on racism and even met with President John F. Kennedy on the subject!

James didn't want to be seen as a leader or an activist, but rather as a witness. His writing on race and sexuality made a difference in American culture with an impact that lasts to the present.

JÓHANNA
SIGURÐARDÓTTIR
Minn tími mun koma!
1942 – Present
ICELAND

JÓHANNA SIGURÐARDÓTTIR

"**M**y time will come!"

That's what Jóhanna said when she didn't reach her goal of becoming the leader of a political party in 1994. And she was right.

Jóhanna served in the Icelandic Parliament for thirty-one years before her time came. She was the longest-serving member of Parliament ever in the world's oldest parliament. She waited and waited, and then in 2009, she rose to become the prime minister of the whole country!

Being prime minister (which is similar to being president) is a big deal, and Jóhanna becoming prime minister was a *really* big deal. Why? Jóhanna was the first woman ever in her country to be prime minister *and* she was the first openly LGBTQ+ person to ever lead a country in the modern world. That's two really big firsts!

There are over two hundred countries in the world, and Jóhanna was the first leader to ever represent the LGBTQ+ community. But even in a country she was in charge of, she wasn't equal.

Jóhanna lived with her partner, a writer, Jónína Leósdóttir. They were joined by something called a civil union because two women weren't allowed to marry each other in Iceland. While Jóhanna was prime minister, Iceland changed the law on June 11, 2010, and LGBTQ+ people were allowed to get married. Jóhanna and Jónína changed their civil union to a marriage on the very first day possible.

Jóhanna finished her time as prime minister in 2013, but she can be with Jónína forever.

JOSÉ
SARRIA
1922 – 2013
UNITED STATES

JOSÉ SARRIA

José led an incredible life as an activist drag queen, even though he never thought that's how his life would turn out.

José was an American tutor for folks learning English, and one of his students was an Austrian, Paul Kolish. They fell in love . . . but José felt drawn to Paul's native Europe after the US entered World War II. José felt like the right thing to do was to join the military, so, a fashionista, he chose the navy because he thought they had the most attractive uniforms! When they didn't accept him (because he was too short), he ended up in the army (such drab uniforms!), serving for five years.

Even after all that time, José and Paul were still in love. They would have gotten married, but that was illegal in the 1940s. Then tragedy struck. On Christmas Day 1947, Paul was driving to see José when a drunk driver hit his car and killed him. José was heartbroken. To add to the devastation, Paul's family didn't allow José to have any of Paul's inheritance. If they had been allowed to get married, José would have gotten everything, but instead Paul's birth family did.

Unsure about what to do with the rest of his life, José took the suggestion of a drag performer friend to enter a drag competition. José came in second and won a contract to perform for two weeks. It was the beginning of the career that would define his life and change many others' lives.

At the Black Cat, a bar in Oakland (across the bay from San Francisco), José lit up the stage in a dress and red high heels. He didn't only entertain, he inspired. He gave speeches to the bar's customers about how it was okay to be gay—something most of them had never heard before from anyone in their life. He even tricked the police one night by having all the drag queens wear pins that said "I am a boy," so they couldn't be accused of fraud, the supposed reason for laws against cross-dressing. None of the queens were arrested that night.

José took his activism a step further and became the first openly gay person to run for office in 1961! José wanted his people to have a voice. He didn't win, but he got thousands of votes that proved it wasn't impossible for a gay person to win. Sixteen years later, **Harvey Milk** would win that seat in the same city of San Francisco.

JOSEPHINE BAKER

1906 – 1975
US/FRANCE

JOSEPHINE BAKER

Working in the theater seemed like a distant dream for Josephine, who grew up in poverty in St. Louis. She started working at the age of eight to help support her family, dropping out of school in the sixth grade. She witnessed terrible discrimination and violence due to racism against black people like her. Luckily, her dream came true when she made it onto the stage at the age of thirteen, thanks to a connection she made while waitressing.

She ended up in New York City and got a big break there as a comedic dancer, crossing her eyes and being silly. At the age of nineteen, she took her act to Paris, where her success grew and grew.

Josephine, who was bisexual, was a star! One of the first things she bought herself was a collection of dolls, something she'd always wanted as a child but could never afford. She also got herself many pets, including a snake, a pig, a goat, and a chimpanzee. She even had a cheetah named Chiquita that she took for walks in its diamond collar.

Then war fell on Europe. Josephine was ready to do her part. Her unique status as a celebrity made her a great spy! She worked for her adopted country of France to find out Nazi information at embassy parties and smuggled secrets in sheets of music. No one suspected a famous dancer of being a government agent. Sneaky!

After World War II, Josephine returned to the United States to find racial discrimination as bad as ever. After being invited into European palaces, she couldn't even go into an American diner to get a coffee because of segregation. Josephine again used her status for good and refused to perform for segregated audiences, forcing businesses to integrate. She worked with the NAACP and even spoke at the 1963 March on Washington.

Josephine adopted thirteen children, and her life was full. The flamboyant icon passed away peacefully in her sleep and twenty thousand people lined the street for her funeral procession, the casket of a national hero draped in the French flag.

Juana Inés de la Cruz

1648–1695
MEXICO

JUANA INÉS DE LA CRUZ

*I*n the shadow of the volcano Popocatépetl, little Juana grew up with a single mom in a small village. Juana had one goal in life: education. She studied all the time and loved learning new things, no matter the subject. She taught herself to read and write on her own by age six or seven. There was one problem: women didn't have a right to education beyond high school in her time and place.

Juana had an idea—she could dress up like a man and go to college that way! Her mom said no way. So Juana had to take matters into her own hands. She kept teaching herself more and more until she was one of the best-educated women in the whole country.

News of this genius spread, and the most powerful man in New Spain (that's what Mexico was called before independence) invited her to the palace for a unique test. He gathered forty of the smartest men in the country to quiz seventeen-year-old Juana to see if any of them could stump her. Questions about science, philosophy, literature, math, and more were lobbed at the young self-taught scholar. She aced every test. Pretty impressive!

Since she couldn't go to college, she took one of her only other options and became a nun. Her life at the convent in Mexico City allowed her to continue her self-education. In between the five daily prayers, she found time to write and then write some more.

She became an extremely gifted poet, now considered one of the best in Spanish of all time. This included writing love poems to women! One line in a poem dedicated to the wife of that powerful man who had set up the test for Juana years ago said "loving you is a crime for which I shall never repent." Juana was an advocate for women's education (which sometimes got her in trouble) but never stopped being herself in her poetry—no matter what.

JULIE

D'AUBIGNY

APPROX. 1673 - 1707
FRANCE

JULIE D'AUBIGNY

Julie drew attention wherever she went, earning her living through both opera singing and sword fighting. Yes, opera singing and sword fighting. Those might seem like two really different paths, but Julie loved them both.

Julie also loved both men and women, and her love sometimes got her into trouble. One time, Julie and her boyfriend had to flee Paris because he had killed a man in an illegal duel by sword. Another time, Julie's girlfriend was put into a convent to be kept away from her . . . so Julie set the convent on fire to stage her girlfriend's escape! Julie was sentenced to death for her crime, so she fled back to Paris. She spent a lot of her life on the run.

Julie, who often wore men's clothes, was eventually pardoned by the king and allowed to join the Paris Opera in 1690. Presenting as androgynous on-stage, Julie made a name for herself as a talented performer but couldn't stay out of trouble.

She kissed a girl at a party one night in 1695 and was challenged to duels by three different men. Julie won all three fights! But duels were illegal in Paris at the time, so the singer once again had to run away to escape the law.

Julie was definitely mischievous but also showed others how to ignore gender expectations hundreds of years before it was acceptable in their culture to do so.

LILI ELBE

1882–1931
DENMARK

LILI ELBE

*T*he female model for the painting Gerda Wegener was working on was running late, and Gerda really needed to work on painting the folds of the dress draped around the shoes. She begged her spouse to step in and help by putting on stockings, a dress, and high heels as a temporary model. Gerda had no idea this would change her spouse's life forever.

Her spouse was a painter as well . . . a *male* painter, they both thought at the time. After much begging, Gerda's spouse reluctantly agreed and donned the women's clothing for the first time, having only dressed as a man up to then. When the model arrived, she suggested Gerda's spouse go by the name Lili, and it stuck.

Everything clicked for Lili as soon as she looked in the mirror. It was like she was always meant to be this way and had always been this way at the same time. Nothing was the same after that day in the early 1910s. Lili began borrowing her wife's clothes and dressing as a woman more and more in private, and then in public too. Over time, she began to want to transition in a way that had never been done before—getting a surgery to give her female external organs.

When she first went to doctors to explore this possibility, they threatened to lock her up for insanity. She was seen as sick, not as a patient deserving of the help she wanted. Thankfully, she found a clinic in Berlin run by **Magnus Hirschfeld**, who was pioneering such physical transitions. Trying the surgeries was dangerous—they were highly experimental. The risk was entirely worth it to Lili—she only wanted to live if she could have the surgeries.

Over a few months in 1930 in Germany, Lili underwent three surgeries between her legs, with Gerda supporting her the whole way. They were a success, and she was delighted! She was one of the first people to ever change her physical sex.

But a year later, she still felt like there was something missing. She wanted a uterus and decided to get a fourth surgery to give her one. Sadly, this procedure was not a success, and Lili passed away from complications due to the surgery. Lili wrote that while fourteen months might not seem like a long time to live fully as yourself, to her it felt like a full lifetime, and she had no regrets.

MA RAINEY

1882 – 1939
UNITED STATES

MA RAINEY

Went out last night with a crowd of my friends
They must've been women, 'cause I don't like no men
It's true I wear a collar and tie . . .
Talk to the gals just like any old man

A woman singing about women like that . . . in 1928?! Ma's song was unlike anything else out there. Her ad for the song above showed Ma in a suit coat talking to two women. She clearly wasn't afraid to show everyone who she was!

By the time the song above came out, Ma was a successful blues singer with Paramount Records. More than that, she was the "Mother of the Blues," so named because she was one of the first ever to record a blues song, in 1923.

Singing the blues meant singing about real life, especially the hard stuff. Growing up in the southern US not long after slavery was abolished, Ma had plenty of hard stuff to sing about. She loved both men and women and sang a lot about the difficulties of relationships, when the top songs of the time were about easy love. Ma was all about keeping it real.

Onstage, Ma was a presence to be reckoned with. You could hear her first—jangling under the weight of her bangles. Her signature gold coin necklace glistened in the lantern light like the sequins of her headband and dress. Although she was short, she filled up the room when she opened her mouth and her deep, beautiful voice sang out.

Ma spent a good part of her life performing on the road, but she found time to mentor other bi blues singers like Bessie Smith. Ma broke the rules and made the rules all at the same time, blazing a trail for any singers today who keep it real.

MAGNUS HIRSCHFELD

Per Scientiam
ad Justitiam

1868 - 1935
GERMANY

MAGNUS HIRSCHFELD

One hundred years before the Stonewall Rebellion, a man was born who would officially begin the struggle for LGBTQ+ rights: Magnus Hirschfeld.

He was born to Jewish parents in a town on the coast of the Baltic Sea that is in modern-day Poland. He always loved school and studying, and he became a doctor who quickly took an interest in patients who were gay like him. They were so sad and desperate in a world that didn't understand them. Magnus wanted to help!

Magnus believed that through his scientific approach, he could convince Germany and the world that LGBTQ+ people deserved equal rights. His logic: every person has their own biological traits, and being LGBTQ+ is just another trait. People had only thought of being LGBTQ+ as a sickness before, but Magnus tried to show it was just another natural part of people.

Magnus went way further than having a theory—he created a whole organization that advocated this idea: the Scientific-Humanitarian Committee. Founded in 1897, this was the world's first LGBTQ+ rights organization! He also founded the important Institute for Sexual Science in 1919. These world-changing organizations were not only firsts but also lifelines for many LGBTQ+ people of the time. Magnus became the go-to person in all of Europe on questions of gender and sexuality. People wrote to him asking for help, and he replied with information they couldn't get anywhere else.

Just when he was making progress on winning legal LGBTQ+ rights in Germany, the country started changing for the worse. The Nazis came to power in 1933, and just a few months into their rule, they ransacked his institute, burning years of carefully compiled research. Magnus's work was mostly destroyed, and the resources he was providing to the LGBTQ+ community ended.

Magnus left Germany because of the rise of the Nazis and passed away while abroad. His work, his progress, and his ideas lived on to inspire the continuation of the LGBTQ+ rights movement in other countries as well as in Germany in the decades after the Nazis were defeated. His gravestone bears his motto: "Through science to justice."

MANVENDRA SINGH GOHIL

1965-Present INDIA

MANVENDRA SINGH GOHIL

Son of the Maharaja of Rajpipla (a prince in Western India), Manvendra was under pressure to live life a certain way. Get married, have kids, yada yada yada. He went along with the plan mapped out for him and married a woman . . . but soon divorced. He just couldn't do it. *Why won't "normal" life work out for me?* he kept wondering. Eventually he realized he's gay. A gay prince in a country where being gay was not accepted? Impossible. Unacceptable. But Manvendra had to find a way.

Manvendra did something really difficult and brave in 2006—he came out! It didn't go well. His parents disowned him. His mother put an ad in the newspaper stating that she didn't support him. People protested in the streets calling for Manvendra to give up the title of prince and be banished. They burned his picture. It seemed like he had lost everything.

Thankfully, Manvendra is very talented when it comes to the media. He did interview after interview, and article by article, the attention being paid to him became more and more positive. A life-changing moment came in 2007, when he was invited to go on *The Oprah Winfrey Show*. (Oprah is very popular in India, so this gave him some good cred.)

With increasingly approving press around India and the whole world, he came to be loved by the public once again. Not only did he find acceptance in India (thanks to some help from **Navtej Johor** and his decriminalization case), but he became a celebrity around the world as the only openly gay prince. He has been a guest of honor at Pride celebrations from Stockholm to São Paulo. Even his dad began to support him.

Then something really special happened. Manvendra's dad donated a fifteen-acre estate in their state of Gujarat for Manvendra to turn into an LGBTQ+ community center in 2018. Manvendra is creating a campus where twenty-five LGBTQ+ people who have been rejected by their families can live and learn professional skills so they can support themselves. There's nothing else like it in all of India.

POWER TO THE PEOPLE!

MARSHA P.
JOHNSON

1945 – 1992
UNITED STATES

MARSHA P. JOHNSON

Marsha was a bright light of Greenwich Village in New York City. She lit up everywhere she went with her big smile and kind personality. She often dressed up with flowers in her hair and fun outfits. Everyone loved Marsha, and she loved everyone.

One time, Marsha was down to her last two dollars and she used it to buy a box of cookies. She gave out all the cookies to others on the street, not leaving any for herself. She knew what it was like to be hungry, and she cared about helping anyone in the same situation, even if she was hungry herself.

Marsha, who was at the 1969 Stonewall Rebellion and maybe even helped start it, was really close friends with **Sylvia Rivera**, and the two of them saw their trans community struggling. So many young trans people in New York City were homeless, and Marsha and Sylvia wanted to give them a place to be safe off the streets. Whenever they got a hotel room, they would sneak kids in—up to fifty people in two hotel rooms at a time!

In 1970, they raised the money to rent a four-bedroom apartment they called STAR House. There was no heat or electricity to start out, but it was more than many who stayed there had had since they'd left their homes. Marsha and Sylvia worked hard to get enough money to keep STAR House open, and they were the very first group to work to help trans homeless youth in New York City. Marsha is remembered as an important activist for the LGBTQ+ community and a loving mother figure for many.

MARTINE

ROTHBLATT

1954 – Present
UNITED STATES

74

MARTINE ROTHBLATT

Martine and her wife, Bina, got terrible news one day in 1994—just about the worst news possible. Their fourth and youngest child, ten-year-old Jenesis, was diagnosed with an incurable disease. The doctors said Jeni had months to live.

Martine was an openly trans CEO (actually the highest-paid female CEO in the world at the time) and entrepreneur (the inventor of satellite radio!) and wasn't one to accept what she was handed. Bina and Martine sought out the best doctors for Jenesis, but they all said that there was nothing that would save her life. Hardly anyone was inventing drugs for rare diseases because you couldn't make enough money off them.

So Martine found a drug that had promise but wasn't being developed and bought it for herself. She studied science textbooks and taught herself what she needed to know to develop the drug for Jenesis. And guess what—she did it! The drug has extended thousands of lives, including Jeni's, who is now in her thirties. Bina and Martine now run a company that creates treatments for rare diseases.

Martine is incredible not just for taking this remarkable initiative as a parent, but as a person making the future come to life in the present. Martine creates human-like robots and has written several books on futuristic ideas she is working on, such as downloading a person's mind like a computer. After so much innovation, who knows what she'll do next!

MARYAM KHATOON MOLKARA

1950 - 2012
IRAN

MARYAM KHATOON MOLKARA

Maryam had known she was a girl for a long time even though she was assigned male at birth. As a little child, she even drew with chalk on her face the way a woman would paint on makeup.

Her parents couldn't accept this, and neither did the people around her in Iran. Maryam suffered for being trans—she was fired from her job, thrown in jail, and forced to take male hormones. It was a terrible time, but Maryam was determined to change her fate and wouldn't give up.

As a devout Muslim, Maryam cared about her religious leaders' opinions on what she should do. She knew she wanted to physically transition, but she wouldn't get gender affirmation surgery without the blessing of an ayatollah (a Muslim leader). So in 1987, she showed up on the doorstep of the powerful Ayatollah Khomeini in Tehran. Can you imagine how scary that must have been?

She was dressed in men's clothing with a pair of shoes draped around her neck, a symbol showing that she was seeking shelter. But when she arrived at the ayatollah's complex, his bodyguards came out and beat her up! She screamed, "I am a woman! I am a woman!" and eventually they brought her inside.

As soon as she had made it through to the ayatollah's home, he came out and spoke with her. He was very open to learning about what she had to say, and he quickly gave her exactly what she had been seeking: a fatwa (a declaration) stating that "sex reassignment, if advised by a reliable doctor, is permissible." Wow!

This opened the door not only for Maryam but for all other trans people in Iran to be able to transition more safely and legally, and without going outside their religious laws. Life continues to be very difficult for LGBTQ+ people in Iran, but what Maryam did was still a huge step forward . . . and showed incredible courage.

NATALIE CLIFFORD BARNEY

1876 – 1972
US / FRANCE

NATALIE CLIFFORD BARNEY

Over two thousand years ago, there was a poet named Sappho who wrote poetry about women's love for other women. No other woman would publish poetry like that until 1900, when Natalie Clifford Barney did.

Natalie was an out and proud lesbian in an era when that wasn't accepted in most circles. Born in Ohio, she lived most of her life in Paris, where she found a community of writers and artists who accepted the LGBTQ+ community. She hosted a famous weekly gathering of these creatives where they discussed their artistic pursuits every Friday for over sixty years.

In 1900, when she published her first book of poetry, her dad found out about it; he bought up all the remaining copies and destroyed them. Yikes! This didn't stop Natalie though. She published her next book under a fake name so that her dad wouldn't find out and her poetry would still get out to the world.

Natalie loved many women, but her longest relationship lasted over fifty years. This life partner was painter Romaine Brooks, who was also an American living in Paris. Natalie had relationships with other women during those fifty-plus years because she was polyamorous. That means she loved more than one person at the same time.

As an author of over a dozen books, Natalie was a respected writer, but maybe more important is how unashamed she was to be a lesbian. Natalie once said "my queerness is not a vice, is not deliberate, and harms no one." This argument that being gay is not a sickness, isn't a choice, and doesn't hurt anyone was ahead of her time. She was an inspiration for many women, even today.

NAVTEJ JOHAR

1959- Present
INDIA

NAVTEJ JOHAR

When Navtej was nineteen, he went to see a performance of Bharatanatyam dance, a traditional Hindu dance that is almost always danced by women. Instantly, he knew that he wanted to try it. Actually, not just try it, but dedicate his whole life to it and totally rock at it. It didn't matter that he was a man or that he was Sikh; he just knew that this was his home.

He did go on to rock at it—so much so that he's now an award-winning world-renowned Bharatanatyam dancer! One day in 1994, a journalist named Sunil Mehra came to see him dance, so he could write a story about him. Sunil was enchanted by the dancer, and the next day, they went for coffee . . . which turned into lunch . . . which turned into dinner. They have been together ever since that date that just wouldn't end.

But in Navtej and Sunil's country of India, their relationship was illegal: being gay was a crime. There's actually a complicated story there: India made being gay legal in 2009 . . . and then changed its mind and made it illegal *again* in 2013! It was a terrible setback for LGBTQ+ people across India.

Navtej decided to *do something* about it. Not just protest, but become the public face of a court case that would go to India's Supreme Court to ask that being gay be legal again! This was a huge decision, but Navtej made it spontaneously over breakfast one day. He just felt it was so completely unacceptable that his relationship with Sunil would be criminal that there was no other choice than to go all the way with making this wrong right.

Navtej, Sunil, and three other LGBTQ+ Indians filed their case in 2016, and in 2018, the Supreme Court ruled in their favor—that means they won! Navtej and Sunil live together happily just like before, but now with a weight off their shoulders.

1583 - 1663
ANGOLA

NZINGA

NZINGA

Nzinga was born with the umbilical cord wrapped around her neck. According to her people, this meant she would grow up to be a proud person. They weren't wrong.

She was born into the royal family of the Ndongo and Matamba kingdoms in southwestern Africa and started her political career when her father allowed her to shadow him in his official affairs even though she wasn't next in line for the throne. When her brother became king, Nzinga, who wore male clothing, was his special diplomat to deal with the Portuguese.

The Portuguese were invading Africa and taking people as slaves. One day in 1622, Nzinga was sent to negotiate with the Portuguese on behalf of her people. When she arrived, the Portuguese negotiator sat in a throne-like chair, and she was told to sit on the floor. Nzinga knew this would indicate she was less powerful than her counterpart, so she signaled for someone from her kingdom to come over to her and kneel on their hands and knees. She sat on their back, using the person like a bench. Together, these two surprised the Portuguese by showing through body language that they were equals, not inferior. Shocked, the Portuguese agreed to Nzinga's terms.

The Portuguese did not honor the agreement and continued to steal people as slaves through raids. (Not really a surprise when you consider the ethics of people doing such things.) When Nzinga became ruler of her people in 1624, she fought fearlessly and tirelessly for decades against the invaders. She kept her people safe as best she could in a scary time and is remembered as a brilliant mind. Nzinga was a warrior who protected her people against slavers until her death at the age of eighty.

PAULI MURRAY

1910 - 1985
UNITED STATES

"ONE PERSON PLUS ONE TYPEWRITER CONSTITUTES A MOVEMENT"

PAULI MURRAY

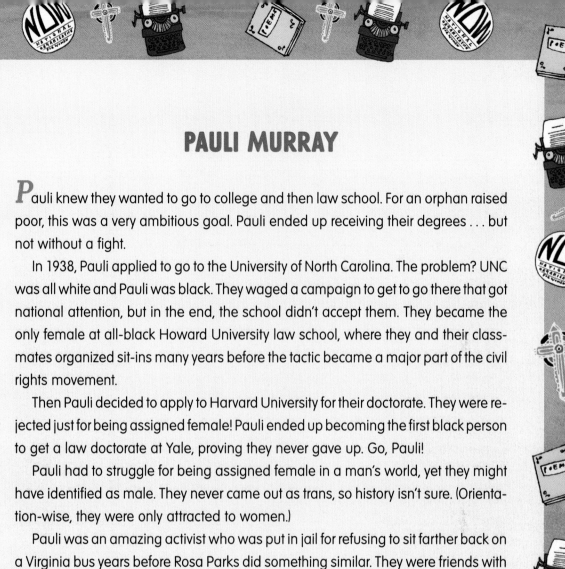

Pauli knew they wanted to go to college and then law school. For an orphan raised poor, this was a very ambitious goal. Pauli ended up receiving their degrees . . . but not without a fight.

In 1938, Pauli applied to go to the University of North Carolina. The problem? UNC was all white and Pauli was black. They waged a campaign to get to go there that got national attention, but in the end, the school didn't accept them. They became the only female at all-black Howard University law school, where they and their class-mates organized sit-ins many years before the tactic became a major part of the civil rights movement.

Then Pauli decided to apply to Harvard University for their doctorate. They were re-jected just for being assigned female! Pauli ended up becoming the first black person to get a law doctorate at Yale, proving they never gave up. Go, Pauli!

Pauli had to struggle for being assigned female in a man's world, yet they might have identified as male. They never came out as trans, so history isn't sure. (Orienta-tion-wise, they were only attracted to women.)

Pauli was an amazing activist who was put in jail for refusing to sit farther back on a Virginia bus years before Rosa Parks did something similar. They were friends with Eleanor Roosevelt and worked for many causes besides racial equality, even helping to create the National Organization for Women. Pauli's writing influenced important cases like *Brown v. Board of Education,* and Justice Ruth Bader Ginsburg has cited their work.

In 1977, Pauli decided it was time for a big change. They changed careers and became an Episcopal priest! They are considered the first ever black assigned-female person to become one. It's amazing that such a trailblazer's name is so little known.

RENÉE RICHARDS

RENÉE RICHARDS

"*R*enée" means "reborn" in French. Renée Richards didn't choose this name by accident.

Renée left New York for California to start over when she transitioned from male to female in 1975. In California, as in New York, she was an ophthalmologist (an eye doctor) who played tennis on the side.

Renée had been a star on the men's tennis team at Yale and in the navy before transitioning, but in California she was starting over with a new name no one knew her by. At a women's tournament in 1976, someone recognized her unique lefty serve, and a scandal broke out. Everyone was upset that someone assigned male at birth was playing as female. Women boycotted playing with her. Renée was a woman who just wanted to keep playing the sport that she loved.

The official tennis organizations banned Renée from playing (if she wouldn't take a test to prove she was a woman), but Renée wasn't about to give up. She sued the United States Tennis Association for the right to play!

No one had ever done anything like that before. Renée said in her case that she had the right to play in the US Open because of an existing law that said you couldn't discriminate based on gender. How would the judge rule?

Well, in 1977 the judge decided that Renée was right! You can't discriminate, and not letting Renée play was discriminating. Renée not only won the right to play in the Women's US Open but also won for trans athletes who came after her. Renée went on to become a pro tennis player until she retired at the age of forty-seven and went back to ophthalmology in New York.

RUDOLF NUREYEV

1938 – 1993
RUSSIA

RUDOLF NUREYEV

Rudolf was born inside a Trans-Siberian train speeding past a lake near Mongolia. Perhaps the rhythm of the wheels stayed with him, because he would grow up to be widely considered the greatest ballet dancer of his time.

Rudolf, who loved both men and women, grew up poor in Ufa, a Russian city closer to Kazakhstan than to Russia's biggest cities, where he longed to go to study dance. His parents, who were Muslims before being assimilated into communist Russia, could only provide a few potatoes a week for their children for food. Rudolf, always hungry, went to school with no shoes and was teased for being different.

He was instantly called to dance the first time he saw it. His teacher in Ufa was impressed with his talent and gave him lessons on a barre made out of a row of movie seats. He began to work himself out of poverty, dancing from bar to bar for coins with an accordion as a partner.

When he was seventeen, Rudolf went to St. Petersburg and was accepted to study ballet full-time, and then he accepted an offer to star in a professional dance company when he graduated. He was a unique dancer who did things his own way, from dance moves to costume choices.

Rudolf's country didn't allow him much freedom, so in 1961 he did something daring and illegal—he left. What he did made international headlines. One day in the Paris airport, he took exactly six steps away from his Russian guards toward the French police and said, "I want to stay in your country." His guards grabbed him, but the French fought for him. Rudolf got to stay in France, but back at home, he was convicted of treason and sentenced to prison. He had to stay away until 1987 to avoid being thrown in jail!

Rudolf's career in dance soared, and he was a global star. Audiences would blanket the stage with flowers and he would come out again and again and again to bow after a performance because they wouldn't stop cheering. He danced for the Royal Ballet in London and directed the Paris Opera Ballet. Before he died of complications due to HIV/AIDS, he transformed the world of dance with his special talent.

SALLY RIDE

1951 - 2012
UNITED STATES

RIDE

90

SALLY RIDE

*H*ave you ever dreamed of becoming an astronaut? Well, in 1983 Sally Ride became the first American woman ever to go to space!

Early on, it looked like Sally might become a tennis player. She loved both science and tennis in high school and didn't know what to choose! Professional tennis player **Billie Jean King** even noticed how good Sally was and encouraged her to go pro like her. However, Sally decided to stay in school.

Sally went to *a lot* more school after high school, even getting her doctorate from Stanford. Then, one day, she saw an ad in the newspaper from the National Aeronautics and Space Administration (NASA), the United States's official space agency. They were looking for future astronauts! Sally applied—and so did eight thousand other people. But Sally's hard work paid off and she was one of thirty-five people (mostly men) accepted into the space program. She trained hard and got to go to outer space—twice!

Sally and her partner, former pro women's tennis player Tam O'Shaughnessy, wrote books about space together too. By going to space, Sally inspired countless young girls to get involved in science, but she wanted to do even more.

Sally and Tam created a foundation called Sally Ride Science that encourages children to learn about science—especially space. Tam is still running the program today, and Sally's legacy of inspiration lives on.

SIMON NKOLI

When Simon joined the Gay Association of South Africa, he didn't really feel welcome. He was a black man in a mostly white organization in a segregated country. But he didn't give up—he started his own subgroup called the Saturday Group that addressed the needs of black members! (Know why it was called the Saturday Group? Yup, they mostly met on Saturdays.)

Simon was an activist for LGBTQ+ rights, racial equality, and other causes. He even spent four years in jail for his activism! He was charged with treason in 1985 for speaking out against apartheid (government-organized segregation). And did that white LGBTQ+ group help him? No. They said they didn't get involved in politics.

When he was finally released from prison, he founded GLOW, the Gay and Lesbian Organisation of the Witwatersrand. Simon and this group did something amazing in 1990—they organized the very first South African Pride!

Around eight hundred people participated in Johannesburg, but some put paper bags over their heads so no one would know who they were. Going to a Pride in 1990 South Africa was risky—no one knew if they would be safe. Simon gave a speech at that Pride, saying, "I am black and I am gay. I cannot separate the two parts of me . . . When I fight for my freedom I must fight for both."

Simon, who was one of the first openly HIV-positive gay black men in his country, worked with Nelson Mandela and many others on South Africa's new constitution as it came out of apartheid. He campaigned for LGBTQ+ protections in this document, and in 1996, South Africa became the first country in the world to have protection from discrimination based on sexual orientation constitutionally guaranteed!

CHRISTOPHER ST

BAR

1920–2014
UNITED STATES

STORME
DELARVERIE

STORMÉ DELARVERIE

*I*magine the biggest stage you can. Well, the Jewel Box Revue was a drag show that played stages like that—the largest venues, like the Apollo Theater and Radio City Music Hall. The show included twenty-five drag queens and one drag king. That drag king was Stormé DeLarverie.

Stormé was a butch lesbian from New Orleans who was bullied as a child for being biracial (her mom was black and her dad was white). Life wasn't easy in the South . . . so she joined the circus as a teenager to get away! She rode jumping horses for Ringling Bros. and Barnum & Bailey Circus.

When she settled in New York City, she joined the Jewel Box Revue. She dressed as a man onstage for audiences of both black people and white people together. (In the 1950s and 1960s, when this was going on, that was a big deal because of segregation.)

Offstage, Stormé did something even more daring. She was one of the first to fight back at the Stonewall Rebellion and helped to start the whole thing! Talk about a big deal.

Stormé worked as security for LGBTQ+ bars in New York until she was eighty-five, making sure people were safe. Even when she wasn't on the job, she patrolled the streets of LGBTQ+ areas and is remembered as a protector of the community. She called the New York City community her "babies," watching over them lovingly and bravely until it was her time to join her girlfriend of over twenty-five years, Diana, who passed in 1969.

SYLVIA RIVERA

1951–2002
UNITED STATES

SYLVIA RIVERA

Sylvia left her home in New Jersey forever when she was just ten years old. Her mother had died when she was three and her grandmother, who she lived with, was cruel. Sylvia would wear makeup outside the house and then take it off before getting home because her grandmother wouldn't approve, since Sylvia was assigned male at birth. She *had* to be herself, so she left for Greenwich Village in New York City.

There, she thankfully found a close-knit community of drag queens and trans women who welcomed her, including the woman who would become her best friend, **Marsha P. Johnson**. Sylvia was a teenager when she and Marsha were at the Stonewall Rebellion of 1969. They fought back against the police, who constantly harassed their LGBTQ+ community. Those riots were an important moment that sparked the modern movement for LGBTQ+ rights.

In the summer after Stonewall, Sylvia got involved with the new LGBTQ+ groups forming in New York City. In 1971, she worked very hard with the group Gay Activists Alliance to get gay and trans rights recognized in the city. But the group decided it would be too hard to get trans rights, so they dropped them and only pursued getting gay rights. It was a really mean move. Sylvia was hurt—her own community had betrayed her.

Sylvia worked the rest of her life for LGBTQ+ rights, including gay rights even though many gay rights activists continued to ignore trans rights (*grr*). Sylvia spoke out about how trans people were experiencing violence and discrimination, and only other trans people seemed to want to help. Sylvia did all she could for trans people who were homeless like she was or in jail often like she was. Her work is so respected today that there is even an organization doing trans rights work that is named after her: the Sylvia Rivera Law Project.

What would you do if the people who you thought were your allies didn't fight for you?

TSHEPO
RICKI
KGOSITAU

1987 – Present
BOTSWANA

TSHEPO RICKI KGOSITAU

Ricki didn't just change her own life on December 12, 2017—she changed the lives of many more. On that day, a high court in her country of Botswana ruled in her favor in a historic case. But we'll hear more about that later.

Before she was making history, Ricki was an energetic fashion-loving child playing house in rural southern Botswana, playing the part of the mommy (raising the curiosity of those around her because she had been assigned male at birth). She loved to steal her grandma's food to pretend to cook, and play with makeup and high heels. When she moved to the capital, Gabarone, her kindergarten teachers called her parents in for a meeting to tell them there was something wrong with their "son," who kept asking to be called a girl.

It took until middle school for Ricki's transition to be respected. Her family got on board, and a supportive teacher encouraged her. In high school, Ricki still had to wear the boys' uniform, but she dressed it up with bangles and wore makeup. It wasn't until she saw Oprah's special on Jazz Jennings on TV that she realized there was a word for who she was: trans.

One day in 2010, Ricki lost her Botswana national ID card. For someone else, getting it replaced would have been a routine inconvenience. However, when Ricki went to get it replaced, she was told that because the lost ID said she was male and she presented as female, they couldn't give her a new one. This inconsistency around her sex on this little piece of laminated paper would turn into a years-long legal battle.

Ricki just wanted her new ID—she needed it for important things like getting a job. But to get it she needed to hire a lawyer and take on the entire government of Botswana! The case became about much more than Ricki's ID—it would go on to affect trans rights in all of Africa. If Ricki won, it would mean no trans person in Botswana would have to go through this ordeal again. And in 2017, she won!

There was one thing left to do that her new female ID opened the door to—get married. Ricki happily wedded her love, Beltony Kanza, in 2018 in Botswana. (Always the fashionista, she designed her wedding dress herself.) This is just the beginning of her life story—and of the struggle for trans rights across her continent.

WEN of HAN

202 – 157 BC
CHINA

WEN OF HAN

During the Han dynasty in ancient China, it was normal for emperors to have a wife and boyfriends and girlfriends all at the same time. Emperor Wen was no exception. He was married to Empress Dou and also loved a man named Deng Tong openly.

One day, the emperor had a dream about a man dressed in a particular robe. When he woke up, he searched and found a man dressed in that exact robe! Wen and Deng Tong were together ever after. Pretty romantic, no? Wen showered his boyfriend in gifts and even gave him the title of lord.

Wen cared about his people and did a lot during his reign to make their lives better. He created a system to give a monthly amount of food to people over the age of eighty, and he reduced taxes for everybody, especially people who didn't have families to help them. He took people's opinions into account, made the punishments for crimes less severe, and didn't waste money on fancy things for himself. He even made peace between his country and a kingdom in the area of present-day Vietnam.

Wen of Han is remembered as one of the kindest rulers of China, who presided over a very stable and prosperous time. And his love for Deng Tong went down in history too.

WE'WHA

1849–1896
UNITED STATES

WE'WHA

Did you know that before Europeans showed up, many places in the world accepted more than two genders? Yup, there used to be many Native Nations who recognized three or four or five or more genders as the norm. It wasn't just within an LGBTQ+ community, but within the Nation as a whole.

We'wha was born into one of those places. The Pueblo of Zuni, located in what is now New Mexico, assigned gender based on how a child acted, who they were as a person, and not just how their body looked. Actually, many Native American tribes saw gender more fluidly than other cultures, and still do today.

We'wha, who would have been assigned male at birth in most other cultures, was a "łamana." In her Pueblo of Zuni community, that means that she was able to carry out not only traditionally male roles but also the traditionally female roles she was drawn to.

Now, another thing to know about We'wha's time is that Native people and European settlers didn't know much about each other. When Presbyterian missionaries arrived in the 1870s, when We'wha was in her twenties, like everyone else she probably wasn't sure what to think of them. We'wha decided to learn English and helped the two groups to get to know each other better. She became an important link for understanding.

In 1886, when she was thirty-six years old, We'wha was invited to travel to Washington, DC, to represent the Pueblo of Zuni and their culture. Can you imagine what it would be like to travel over two thousand miles with no airplane or car? We'wha had quite a journey going from New Mexico to Washington, DC. She had never left New Mexico before, so seeing green forests and big cities was all brand-new to her.

We'wha shared her talents in many crafts in DC. Her weavings and pottery were displayed in the National Museum, and she starred in a dance put on at the National Theater that the president, Grover Cleveland, attended. While the European settlers didn't always continue to treat her with respect, We'wha did all she could to build compassion.

A TIMELINE OF LGBTQ+ HISTORY

Note: Pre-1492 to the 20th century: The precolonial world has a wealth of LGBTQ+ diversity. What is considered "normal" for genders and sexualities varies greatly from culture to culture across all inhabited continents before European standards are imposed.

BC era: Several cave paintings and other ancient representations have been found from this time period showing LGBTQ+ people. Sappho writes about female-female love, and Catullus and others write about male-male love.

27 BC – AD 476: Roman Empire. Bisexuality is common, and multiple Roman emperors marry men publicly.

476–1492: Middle Ages. LGBTQ+ people are used as scapegoats for society's problems and as a result are often executed.

1300–1600: Renaissance. Many LGBTQ+ artists contribute to this artistic time period in Europe, including Leonardo da Vinci.

1428–1521: Aztec Empire. The Aztecs punish same-sex acts by death.

1478–1834: Spanish Inquisition. Over 1,600 people are investigated for homosexuality; many are punished for it, including being put to death.

1740: China criminalizes homosexuality for the first time in the country's history.

1791: France decriminalizes homosexuality, the first European country to do so. This also applies to all French-controlled territories overseas.

1815–1914: Height of British Empire. The UK conquers much of the world and brings its anti-LGBTQ+ laws with it. Of the countries where anti-LGBTQ+ laws are still on the books, more than half retain those laws from when they were British colonies.

1869: The word "homosexuality" is first publicly printed in Germany.

1871: Britain's Criminal Tribes Act goes into effect in India. One of the groups it criminalizes are the hijra, a South Asian gender that has existed since ancient times. Today the hijra have legal recognition in India, Nepal, Bangladesh, and Pakistan.

1873: Japan criminalizes homosexuality for the first time in the country's history.

1897: Magnus Hirschfeld founds the Scientific-Humanitarian Committee in Germany, considered the world's first LGBTQ+ rights advocacy group.

1916: Charles Webster Leadbeater founds the Liberal Catholic Church in Australia, considered the first religious group to minister openly to gay men and lesbians.

1918–1937: Harlem Renaissance. A time of incredible African American contributions to the arts. It includes many LGBTQ+ artists, such as Langston Hughes.

1924: The Society for Human Rights is founded in Chicago, the first LGBTQ+ rights organization in the Americas. While this organization only lasted a few months, it paved the way for longer-lasting groups to be founded in the 1950s.

1933–1945: Nazis control Germany. It is estimated that over fifty thousand men are sent to concentration camps for loving men.

1965: A small group of people pickets Independence Hall in Philadelphia, considered to be one of the first public demonstrations for LGBTQ+ rights.

1967: The group Nuestro Mundo is founded in Argentina, considered the first LGBTQ+ rights group in Latin America.

1969: The Stonewall Rebellion happens in New York City, a huge riot that sparks the modern LGBTQ+ rights movement. Canada decriminalizes homosexuality.

1970: The first Pride is organized in New York City as a celebration of the anniversary of the Stonewall Rebellion.

1972: Sweden becomes the first country in the world to allow people to legally change their sex.

1981: HIV/AIDS epidemic begins. Nearly half a million people die of complications due to HIV/AIDS by the year 2000. Today, people living with HIV/AIDS can lead full lives.

1996: South Africa's new constitution says that no one can discriminate against someone for being LGBTQ+, the first national constitution in the world to do so.

2001: The Netherlands legalizes marriage equality, the first country in the world to do so.

2003: Alex McFarlane (an intersex person) receives an Australian passport and birth certificate with the gender marker "X" instead of "M" or "F."

2018: The Supreme Court of India strikes down a colonial-era anti-homosexuality law.

GLOSSARY

The terms used in the LGBTQ+ community are as diverse as its people. The definitions provided here are not definitive. Each term means something personal to each individual and may not be the same as what is listed below. Language is always changing, just like us!

Activist: A person who works for change. Bayard Rustin, Simon Nkoli, and Sylvia Rivera are some examples of activists in this book.

Agender: Not identifying as any gender.

AIDS *(see HIV)*

Androgynous: Appearing not entirely male and not entirely female but somewhere in between or completely outside of those two options.

Asexual (ace): Not having any or having very low desire for sex or sexual partners.

Assigned at birth: When a doctor sees a vagina on a baby and says, "It's a girl," or sees a penis and says, "It's a boy." Sometimes a baby doesn't have what is clearly a penis or vagina and the doctor will make an assignment anyway. The doctor is always just making a guess and doesn't know the gender identity of the baby.

Bisexual (bi): Attracted to members of the same gender and also to people of other genders. The attraction is not necessarily split evenly between people of male and female genders and does not have to be restricted to people of only male and female genders.

Cisgender: A person whose gender identity matches up with the biological sex they were assigned at birth. Example: when the doctor says, "It's a boy!" and then the child grows up to feel like a man inside.

Coming out: When someone tells people that they are LGBTQ+.

Discrimination: Unfair treatment of certain people just because of who they are.

Drag: Dressing as a different sex or gender than you identify as for a performance.

Gay: Someone who is exclusively attracted to people of the same sex or gender.

Gender/Gender identity: How someone identifies internally (examples: man, woman, gender-queer, etc.). Different from "sex," which is biological (examples: male, female, intersex, etc.) and refers to physical characteristics. People can identify with no gender (agender), two genders (bigender), changing between genders (genderfluid), or many other possibilities. Many cultures and countries have their own sets of genders different from those just listed, like the muxe of Mexico, kathoey of Thailand, and bakla of the Philippines.

Gender affirmation surgery: Any surgery that helps a trans person feel more comfortable in their body. Surgeries can be one part of a physical transition, but whether or not someone chooses to have any gender affirmation surgeries does not make them more or less of the gender they identify as.

Heterosexuality: Being straight.

Homophobia (biphobia, transphobia): Disliking gay people (or bi people or trans people) just because they are gay (or bi or trans). Not cool!

Homosexuality: Being gay.

HIV (HIV/AIDS): HIV is the virus that leads to the AIDS disease. Someone can have HIV without having AIDS. HIV/AIDS appeared in the 1980s and took the lives of many LGBTQ+ people, though you don't have to be LGBTQ+ to have it. Today there are treatments for HIV that allow people living with it to lead a full life.

In the closet: Not having come out yet (see *Coming out*).

Integrated: *(see Segregation)*

Intersex: Someone whose combination of physical characteristics (chromosomes, hormones, internal and external reproductive organs, etc.) isn't exclusively male or female. For example, Lili Elbe was born with both testes and ovaries, so she was intersex.

Lesbian: A woman or nonbinary person attracted to women or nonbinary people.

LGBTQ+: Lesbian, gay, bisexual, transgender, queer/questioning. In this book, we use this shortened abbreviation to refer to all LGBTQ+ people including asexual and intersex people.

Marriage equality: When everyone can marry the person they love, including a man marrying a man or a woman marrying a woman. Some places that don't allow full marriage equality do have "civil unions" and/or "domestic partnerships," which have some but not all of the rights, privileges, and responsibilities of marriage (and, of course, not the name).

Nonbinary: An umbrella term for people who do not identify as either male or female; a similar term is "genderqueer." Also a gender identity in itself.

Nonviolence/Nonviolent: Using protests that don't include violence to get what you want. Bayard Rustin is an example of someone who used nonviolence.

Out: Having shared that you are LGBTQ+ with people in your life or even with the public. "To out someone" means to do this without the person's permission (never do this!).

Pansexual: Attracted to people regardless of gender.

Polyamorous: When someone openly has multiple partners at the same time.

Present/Presentation: When someone presents as a certain gender, it means they are letting people know that gender by their appearance, words, or actions.

Pride: Pride is a special holiday for the LGBTQ+ community around the world. It is traditionally celebrated in June because the Stonewall Rebellion happened in June.

Queer: This word started off as a hateful slur against LGBTQ+ people, but was reclaimed starting in the 1990s as a proud identity label. It is sometimes used as an umbrella term referring to all LGBTQ+ people at once and it is sometimes used individually as a way to identify as not straight and/or not cisgender. It means a lot of different things to different people, and some people still associate it with being anti-LGBTQ+.

Segregation: Separating people based on race. Josephine Baker, Bayard Rustin, and Simon Nkoli are some of the LGBTQ+ people in this book who worked for integration, the opposite of this form of discrimination.

Sex: Sex is different from "gender." Sex means male, female, or intersex, usually referring to how someone was assigned at birth. Gender is how someone feels and knows they are inside, even if that is not the same as their sex.

Straight: Someone who is exclusively attracted to people of a different sex or gender.

They/Them: Gender-neutral version of singular pronouns like "he," "him," "she," "her." When we use they/them pronouns for a person in this book, it is because it is the closest match we have in our modern language, not because they necessarily used those pronouns in their time.

Transgender (trans): A person whose gender identity does not match up with the biological sex they were assigned at birth. Example: when the doctor says, "It's a boy!" and then the child grows up to feel like a woman inside. An umbrella term encompassing many identities, including transsexual.

Transition: When someone changes physically and/or socially from one gender to another.

Two-Spirit: Indigenous peoples from Native Nations recognize many different genders. "Two-spirit" is a modern, intertribal umbrella term, created in the 1990s by Native people, to bridge Indigenous and western ideas of gender and sexuality. If We'wha was alive today, her identity as "łamana," a Nation-specific term, would be included under this new, two-spirit umbrella.

PRIDE FLAGS

Pride flags have become a universal symbol of LGBTQ+ identity and community . . . and they keep evolving!

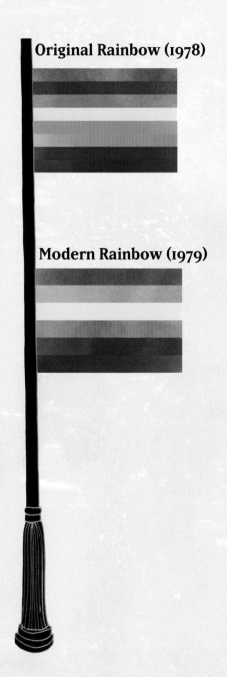

IDENTITY FLAGS

While the LGBTQ+ community can be united in many ways, it's made up of people of dozens of unique identities. Here are specific flags for a few of them:

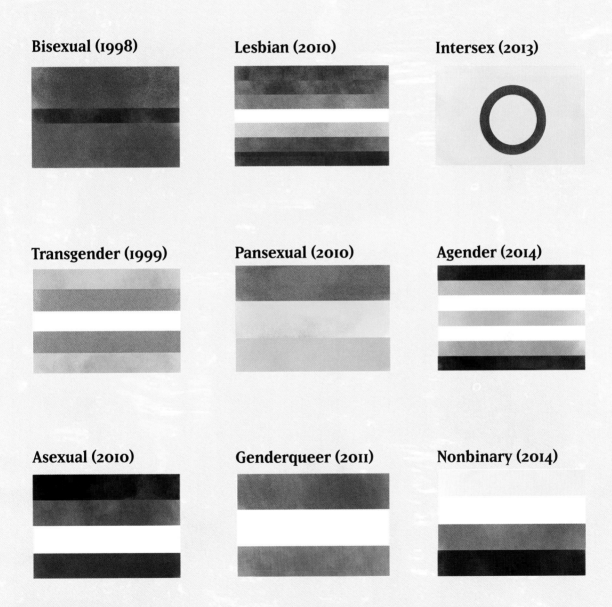

Bisexual (1998)

Lesbian (2010)

Intersex (2013)

Transgender (1999)

Pansexual (2010)

Agender (2014)

Asexual (2010)

Genderqueer (2011)

Nonbinary (2014)

LGBTQ+ SYMBOLS

Before the Pride flag was created in 1978, LGBTQ+ people had many other ways to identify each other and show their pride. Here are just a few, many of which are still in use today.

These interlocking male symbols represent pride of men who love men.

These interlocking female symbols represent pride of women who love women.

This is a transgender pride symbol.

Originally used to identify homosexual prisoners in Nazi concentration camps, the pink triangle was reclaimed as a gay pride symbol in the 1970s.

Originally used to identify certain prisoners in Nazi concentration camps, the black triangle was reclaimed as a lesbian pride symbol in the 1970s.

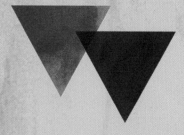

The "biangles" are a bisexual pride symbol, based on the pink triangle.

The labrys (an ancient double-headed ax) has been a lesbian symbol since the 1970s.

This lowercase Greek letter lambda became an LGBTQ+ symbol starting in the 1970s.

This bisexual pride symbol was made as an alternative to the "biangles" that used symbolism from Nazi history.

Oscar Wilde regularly wore a green carnation on his suit to signal homosexuality, popularizing it as a symbol for 1890s men. Other flowering plants with LGBTQ+ associations include violets, lavender, calami, and pansies.

SELECTED BIBLIOGRAPHY

Ailey, Alvin, with A. Peter Bailey. *Revelations: The Autobiography of Alvin Ailey.* Secaucus, NJ: Birch Lane Press, 1995.

American Masters: Billie Jean King. Directed by PBS. Produced by New Black Films. PBS, 2013.

Baldwin, James, with Quincy Troupe. *James Baldwin: The Last Interview and Other Conversations.* Brooklyn, NY: Melville House Publishing, 2014.

Beyer, Georgina, with Cathy Casey. *Change for the Better: The Story of Georgina Beyer as Told to Cathy Casey.* Auckland, NZ: Random House New Zealand, 1999.

Burke, Glenn, with Erik Sherman. *Out at Home: The True Story of Glenn Burke, Baseball's First Openly Gay Player.* New York: Berkley Books, 1995.

Carter, David. *Stonewall: The Riots that Sparked the Gay Revolution.* New York: St. Martin's Press, 2004.

Christina, Queen of Sweden. *Maxims of a Queen, Christina of Sweden (1626–89).* London: Forgotten Books, 2012.

Davis, Angela Y. *Blues Legacies and Black Feminism: Gertrude "Ma" Rainey, Bessie Smith, and Billie Holiday.* New York: Pantheon Books, 1998.

D'Emilio, John. *Lost Prophet: The Life and Times of Bayard Rustin*. New York: University of Chicago Press, 2004.

Elbe, Lili. *Man into Woman: An Authentic Record of a Sex Change*. Edited by Niels Hoyer. New York: E. P. Dutton, 1933.

Gohil, Manvendra Singh. Video interview. February 24, 2019.

Gorman, Michael R. *The Empress Is a Man: Stories from the Life of José Sarria*. Binghamton, NY: Harrington Park Press, 1998.

Herrera, Hayden. *Frida: A Biography of Frida Kahlo*. New York: Harper & Row, 1983.

Hodges, Andrew. *Alan Turing: The Enigma*. Princeton, NJ: Princeton University Press, 1983.

Hoffman, Paul. *Wings of Madness: Alberto Santos-Dumont and the Invention of Flight*. New York: Hyperion, 2003.

Johar, Navtej. Email interview. April 3, 2019.

Jones, Cleve. *When We Rise: My Life in the Movement*. New York: Hachette Books, 2017.

Kavanagh, Julie. *Nureyev: The Life*. New York: Pantheon, 2007.

Kgositau, Tshepo Ricki. Video interview. January 20, 2019.

Lawson, L. P. *Also Known as Albert D. J. Cashier: The Jennie Hodgers Story, or How One Young Irish Girl Joined the Union Army during the Civil War*. Chicago: Compass Rose Cultural Crossroads, 2005.

Murray, Pauli. *Song in a Weary Throat: Memoir of an American Pilgrimage*. New York: Liveright, 2018.

Paz, Octavio. *Sor Juana, or, The Traps of Faith*. Translated by Margaret Sayers Peden. Cambridge, MA: Belknap Press of Harvard University Press, 1988.

Richards, Renée, with John Ames. *Second Serve: The Renée Richards Story*. New York: Stein and Day, 1983.

Shilts, Randy. *The Mayor of Castro Street: The Life and Times of Harvey Milk*. New York: St. Martin's Press, 1982.

Woodhead, Henry. *Memoirs of Christina, Queen of Sweden*. 2 vols. London: Hurst and Blackett, 1863.

ABOUT THE AUTHOR

Sarah Prager is the author of _Queer, There, and Everywhere: 23 People Who Changed the World_ (Harper, 2017), an award-winning book for young adults that you should totally read when you're a teen or adult! It tells stories of people from LGBTQ+ history just like this book, but goes into more depth about their lives. Sarah is also the creator of Quist, a free mobile app that teaches LGBTQ+ and HIV/AIDS history, and a speaker on LGBTQ+ history who visits schools and groups around the world. Sarah lives with her wife and their two children in Massachusetts. You can follow Sarah on Facebook (@sarahprager), Twitter (@Sarah_Prager), and Instagram (@sarahpragerbooks) and visit her at www.sarahprager.com.

Sarah would like to thank Nancy Inteli, Liz Prager, Carrie Howland, Sarah Papworth, Alison Klapthor, Renée Cafiero, Manny Blasco, Gaines Blasdel, Syd Rosen, Sara Franklin, Sara Sargent, Rich Prager, Bev Prager, Terry Landau, Elise McMullen-Ciotti, Curtis Quam, the Pueblo of Zuni, and all fifty people profiled in this book.

ABOUT THE ILLUSTRATOR

Sarah Papworth is an illustrator and textile designer who enjoys drawing and painting, growing vegetables in her garden, practicing yoga, and upcycling her home. She is the illustrator for *I Know a Woman: The Inspiring Women Who Have Shaped Our World* by Kate Hodges and the sequel, *I Know an Artist* by Susie Hodge, among others. Sarah has also enjoyed creating work for companies such as the *Washington Post*, L'Oreal Paris, American Greetings, Royal Botanical Kew Gardens, Quarto, and Scholastic. Sarah lives in a village with her partner in the North Cotswolds, UK. She hopes to one day move to the sea and spend her days painting and drawing from a room with a view, sipping cups of chamomile tea. You can learn more about her at www.sarahpapworth.co.uk, and she spends most of her time on Instagram under @sarahpapworthdesign.

For all their guidance and support throughout the project, Sarah would like to warmly thank Alison Klapthor, Nancy Inteli, and the rest of the team at HarperCollins; Juls Hastings; Lilla Rogers; and Susan McCabe; along with all the studio ladies at Lilla Rogers Studios.

And to the fifty people illustrated: I loved getting to know each person I illustrated—thank you for the inspirational stories!